the library of african american arts and culture

jazz tap

From african drums to american feet

the library of african american arts and culture

jazz tap

From african drums to american feet

anne e. johnson

rosen publishing group, inc./new york

Published in 1999 by The Rosen Publishing Group, Inc.
29 East 21st Street, New York, NY 10010

Copyright © 1999 by The Rosen Publishing Group, Inc.

First Edition

Library of Congress Cataloging-in-Publication Data

Johnson, Anne E.
    Jazz tap : from African drums to American feet / Anne E. Johnson.
        p. cm. -- (The library of African American arts and culture)
    Includes bibliographical references (p.   ) and index.
    ISBN 0-8239-1856-4 (lib. bdg.)
    1. Jazz tap--History. 2. Afro-American dance--History. 3. Dance, Black--History. I. Title. II. Series.
GV1794.5.J65 1998
796.7'8--dc21
98-29523
CIP

Manufactured in the United States of America

Contents

Introduction

De BOP! De BOP! Shoo-be-de BOP! Listen to that rhythm! It moves like jazz music. It has a strong beat like rap. It's fast and complicated, like African drums.

Do you see the guy making those rhythms? He hasn't got a drum. What he has are his own two feet and a corner on the sidewalk. He's hunched over and concentrating hard. His legs are loose. His feet move so quickly that you cannot keep track of them. He's a tap dancer. He can play music with his shoes.

Maybe tap dancing makes you think of Broadway. It may remind you of the Rockettes, who dance in a chorus line at the Macy's Thanksgiving Day Parade. Or you might associate tap dancing with old movie musicals and actors such as Fred Astaire. But did you know that there is also hip-hop tap? And electric synthesized tap? Tap dancing takes all shapes and styles.

You can tap to any music or make your own music with your feet. Tap shoes are like

drums. They are instruments of
rhythm. Since every kind of music
has rhythm, people tap to every-
thing: rap, rock, jazz, blues,
and even classical music.

Jazz tap, also called
rhythm tap, is a style of
tap that began in the
1920s. In jazz tap
a dancer is like a
musician. The
dancer uses
his or her own
feet as an instrument to create
rhythms. In show tap, or Broadway
tap, the way the dance steps look
and the way they are arranged is
very important. But in jazz tap, the
focus is on creating music. In fact,
jazz tap dancers can dance without
any outside music, simply creating a
rhythm with their fancy footwork.

Jazz music inspired the development
of jazz tap. The two art forms share
many traits. Just like a jazz musician,
a jazz tap dancer has the freedom to
invent things as he or she goes along. Tap is also similar

to jazz music in that it was invented in America, but much of its origins can be traced to Africa.

When Africans were forced to come to America as slaves, they brought ideas about rhythm and dance from their native lands. They were denied their freedom, but they preserved their spirit and culture by

keeping alive the rich African tradition of music and dance. When African Americans came into contact with other ethnic groups in the United States, especially the Irish, their ideas and cultures mingled. Tap dance was born from this meeting of different cultures many years ago. It is still growing today.

9

1 seeing the rhythm: dances of west africa

No two people agree on exactly how tap dance began. However, everyone's version of the story starts in the same place: West Africa. Song, music, and dance are so closely connected in Africa that there are words to indicate the combination of all three.

In many cultures, especially African ones, music and dance are combined into one art form. That practice has carried over into tap dancing. Tap is an unusual dance form because it can be both seen and heard. Just like the dances of West Africa, it is movement and music all in one.

The importance of rhythm in jazz tap also has African roots. Rhythm is a musical pattern of regularly recurring sounds, or beats. These beats can either be stressed or unstressed, long or short. In West Africa the rhythm of the drum guides, inspires, and interacts with the dancers. Most West Africans dance barefoot and stomp on the ground

Wahutu tribesman dancing on the shores of Lake Tanganyika in Myanza, Africa

in simple rhythms to the beat of the drum. When an African dancer touches her foot to the ground, she is connecting spiritually with the rhythms of the drum. These dancers do not wear tap shoes or make fancy-sounding rhythms with their feet. However, they always dance to the music of drummers, who play complicated rhythms much like those a tap dancer makes with her feet.

Talking Drums

dza dza! dza dza! dza dza!
 de•gi•de ga•de•dzi! de•gi•de dzi dza!
gi•de•gi•de ga•to! de•gi•de•gi•de dzi dza!

To most ears, this sounds like a complicated drum-beat from an unfamiliar culture. But to people who have heard it since childhood, the drums are not only creating music; they are also "talking." A skilled drummer can communicate through his instrument by using rhythms. When you speak in any language, words come out in a natural rhythm. Drummers play a rhythm that sounds like a sentence. People memorize certain sounds and rhythms, which stand for specific words. Once they do this, they can understand what the drum is saying.

Many West African languages add meaning to

12

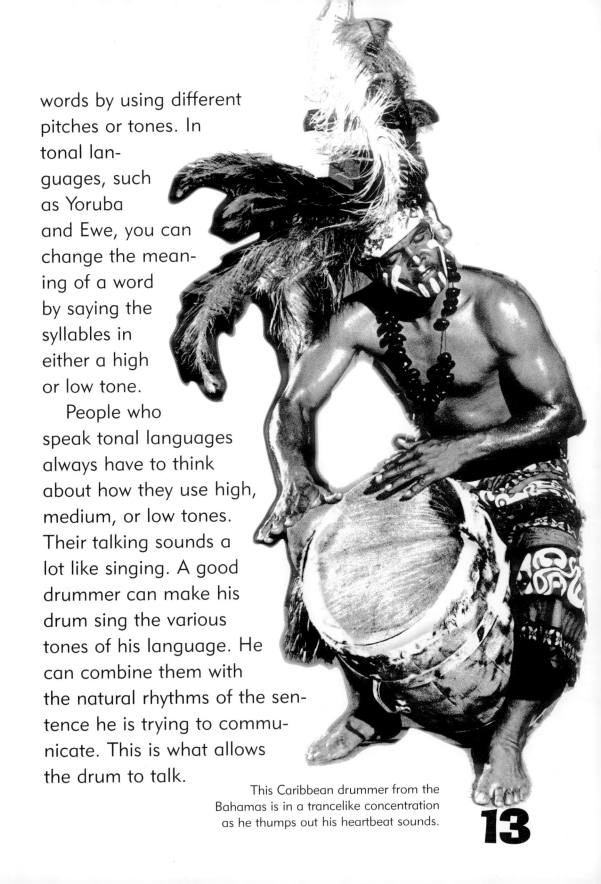

words by using different pitches or tones. In tonal languages, such as Yoruba and Ewe, you can change the meaning of a word by saying the syllables in either a high or low tone.

People who speak tonal languages always have to think about how they use high, medium, or low tones. Their talking sounds a lot like singing. A good drummer can make his drum sing the various tones of his language. He can combine them with the natural rhythms of the sentence he is trying to communicate. This is what allows the drum to talk.

This Caribbean drummer from the Bahamas is in a trancelike concentration as he thumps out his heartbeat sounds.

The dances of West Africa are based on the cycle of life. They are a way to celebrate life's different stages and to communicate with gods and the spirits of ancestors. The rhythm that propels a dance is itself repetitive and cyclical, just like life. A person who joins a dance circle joins in the spiritual power of her ancestors.

The Cycle of Life

In most African cultures, people stand in a circle to dance. The circle may represent the cycle of life. Dancers move in a counterclockwise direction while they shuffle rhythmically with their bare feet. Some

Women's dances are a vital part of African culture. Among the Kuba, the king's many wives are particularly important as keepers of history.

people believe that African dancers keep their feet close to the ground in order to feel the spiritual power of Mother Earth. This shuffle, so popular in African dance, is also the most basic step in tap dancing.

The Challenge Dance

The challenge dance is an African tradition in which dancers compete with each other to be the best. It has also become one of the oldest, most popular forms of rhythm tap. In a challenge dance, several dancers in a circle keep the music going. They do this with their feet or by chanting. They take turns moving into the middle of the circle to show off their very best steps.

In traditional African cultures and in jazz tap, challenge dances show off the strength and speed of the dancer as he tries to outdo his rivals. Challenge dances are also a great way for dancers to learn new steps by watching each other. Rather than copy the steps of their favorite performers, tap dancers borrow and build on one another's steps. They get ideas from other dancers and make the steps come out in their own unique way.

Movements and Music

Tap steps interact with and feed off of the rhythm in music, or they create their own rhythm. The rhythms of tap dance are at least as important as the movements themselves. You can see and hear a tap dancer; he

15

paints a picture with his movements and composes music with his feet. The idea of hearing a dance, instead of just seeing it, is very African. Dance and music are inseparable in many African cultures.

Tap Shoes and Basket Rattles

Most African dancers also use rhythm to make the drumbeat clearer to the listeners. The dancers do not wear tap shoes, but they still find ways to make their rhythms heard.

Tap shoes have pieces of metal called taps attached to the heels and toes that make a loud *crack* when they hit the ground.

Basket rattles are the favorite method. African dancers weave long leaves into tiny baskets. They fill these baskets with pebbles and then tie them to their legs or wrists. Every time they step, the rattles shake. The Igbo sometimes cover their dance costumes with a long dried grass called raffia. Every movement makes a *shushush* sound.

Instead of basket rattles, tap dancers wear tap

Creating Visual Rhythm

Dancers use movement to create visual rhythm—rhythm that you can see. No one can move her whole body as fast as a drummer can play, so a dancer will choose certain parts of a drummer's pattern to emphasize with movement. She might thrust out a hip, slink her shoulders up and down, or jut out her head from side to side. An African dancer learns what parts of the drum pattern to use to keep the visual rhythm of her dance propelling forward.

Dancers can also create visual rhythm through pantomime. Pantomime is rhythmic movement that imitates something. Both African dances and American slave dances often imitated animals. For example, African American slaves would mimic a buzzard in a dance called the Buzzard Lope to celebrate a good crop. The dancers would move in a circle, in the African style, and jerk their heads forward in a pecking motion. Other examples of animal dances by African American slaves were the Turkey Trot, Snake Hips, Mosquito Dance, Fish Tail, and Camel Walk.

A child from the Republic of Dahomey is dancing the frantic "Aguela ye ye" to celebrate traditional holidays.

Wahutu tribesmen dancing with rattles on their ankles

shoes. But the shoes act in a similar way. Tap shoes have an aluminum plate (called a tap) attached by screws to the heel and toe of their leather soles. Their sound varies from one dancer to another depending upon the tightness of the screws and the brand of shoe. In this way they can be "tuned."

Tap shoes work like leg rattles because they make a sound every time the dancer's shoe hits the floor. They also function like drums. A tapper can make patterns as complicated as those of a drummer's. He can move

Polyrhythm

African drummers learn to both hear and play more than one rhythm at the same time. The rhythms they play together may be very different from one another. Polyrhythm, more than one rhythm, takes a lot of practice to play and understand.

in one rhythm and tap in a different one. This means that tap dancers, like African dancers, can create polyrhythm. Tap dancers can also make music to take the place of drummers.

One of the closest connections between African dance and tap is improvisation. Improvisation means dancing spontaneously without following a set routine. In an African dance circle, dancers move into the middle one by one to dance alone. The rhythm of the drummers stays the same, but the dancer can use any movements he wants that fit the beat. In jazz tap, too, a dancer learns how to make up a rhythm on the spot.

Jazz tap is partly a technical skill, but it is also a form of self-expression that comes from the soul of the dancer. When a tap dancer follows his feelings and gets into a groove, he can take the rhythm anywhere he wants. He becomes a musician, free to create a different rhythm or change the tempo at any point. A great dancer can use his talent and knowledge to express his own ideas through rhythm.

Where Does Tap's Feel Come From?

Dance historians sometimes try to be very specific about where tap gets its feel. Some say that the movement of the hips comes from the Sherbo of Sierre Leone. The Congolese also sway their hips and roll their bellies in ways that are similar to those in tap. Perhaps shoulder movements, known in tap as the shimmy, are from the Ibibio of Nigeria. Or they may come from the peoples of Dahomey.

In other words, it may not be possible to say who gave what movements to American tap dance. We do know this: African dance often is set apart from other dance forms because the

This Watusi dancer twists his hips and shoulders with energetic movements that can be found in tap.

dancers have such free, fluid movement in their bodies. These dancers seem to be a part of the earth's energy. It is this energy and freedom of movement, so popular in African dance, that has been passed on to jazz tap.

20

2 finding a new rhythm: african slaves in america

The original journey of African rhythms to America was a difficult and dangerous one. The rhythms traveled with Africans who were taken to America to be sold as slaves. Remembering the music and dance of their native land gave hope and strength to these people who were forced to make America their new home.

A Long, Cruel Journey

Most of the African slaves in America came from West Africa. Their shipboard voyage from Africa to America was called the Middle Passage.

The Middle Passage was a horrible journey. It was long and dangerous, lasting anywhere from fifteen days to four months. Slave traders packed their ships with a cargo of living human beings.

The human figures in this diagram of a slave ship show how slave traders measured the amount of cargo space their vessels had by how many people they could take from Africa to America.

European slave traders did not think that Africans were like other people. Instead, they considered them primitive and childlike creatures. The mystic beauty of African rhythms and dance frightened and fascinated the slave traders. Many wrote in their diaries about their victims' exotic dances.

Some slave traders actually used dancing to steal slaves away from Africa. The traders would invite a group of dancers and drummers on board their ship to entertain the sailors. The Africans would do warrior and ring dances. The sailors would show off British hornpipes and jigs. After a long night, the Africans would lie down on the deck to sleep. The next morning they would find, to their horror, that the ship they were on was out at sea. They would be far from their home-land, headed to the American slave market.

Keeping Tradition Alive

Once they arrived at the plantations, or large farms, in America, African slaves took up singing, drumming, and dancing again. In America many Protestant slave owners believed that dancing was sinful, and they dis-approved of it. But out in the fields of large plantations and in the slave quarters, slaves could not be carefully monitored, and African Americans found ways to keep the tradition of African music and dance alive.

African music and dance were an important part of slaves' lives. Slaves could not complain about their dreadful circumstances to their owners without fear of severe punishment or even death. Music and dance were the best ways of expressing their sorrows. These activities were a source of joy in an otherwise miserable existence.

Dance and music continued to be an important part of life for African slaves in America.

Slave dances on the plantations were much more than simply African ethnic dances. Many new influences affected their dancing and music. Although African movements and rhythms were still a big part of the dances, slaves were in a new land and leading a very different life than before. The dances quickly changed from being African to something else—African American.

Caribbean Influences

Contact with Caribbean blacks was a big influence on American plantation dances. Slave traders often took slaves to the Caribbean before selling them in America to increase their chances of survival. The traders were interested in the slaves' health because the sale of healthy slaves brought them more profit. They believed that the Caribbean culture was somewhere between African and American culture. They thought that by stopping in the Caribbean first, they would help slaves get used to their new surroundings. That way, life in America would not shock their systems too much.

For hundreds of years, slave traders had sold slaves to the French colonists in Haiti, a Caribbean island. When the American slave trade began, a long tradition of slave dancing already existed in the Caribbean. There slaves had the freedom to dance.

Slaves bound for North America, where dancing was often forbidden, were able to learn new styles of dance during their time in the Caribbean. They then carried that knowledge with them to America.

Black Haitians had learned to copy French aristocratic dances. However, they did them with an unmistakably African feel. The calenda was one dance that captured Africans learned from the Caribbean slaves and brought to America. In the calenda a line of men would face a

The ballroom dancing of the French aristocracy was adopted and changed by African and Afro-Caribbean slaves.

line of women. They would repeatedly move toward each other and then retreat, touching each other's thighs every time they met.

A French couple dancing at the time of Louis XV

White Influences

Contact with whites was a big influence on slave dancing. For the slaves, holding a dance was a welcome way to relax and socialize after being forced to work all day in the fields.

The cakewalk, for example, was a competitive plantation dance where couples strutted around and performed complicated steps with a bucket of water on their heads. Whoever succeeded in spilling the least amount of water was awarded a prize of a cake by the plantation owner. Later, dancers abandoned the bucket of water, and the cakewalk evolved into a stage dance.

New styles of dance were emerging among the slaves. They combined the ethnic African dances with the French-influenced dances of Caribbean slaves. To all of this, they added aspects of dances done by white Americans. Little by little the slaves' traditional African dances began to change.

An African American couple dancing at a festival incorporates elements of European dance into their African-influenced style.

bottle caps between your toes: how tap grew up

One of the most important events in tap history took place in 1739, when a slave revolt known as the Cato Conspiracy occurred on a plantation called Stono in South Carolina. Under the leadership of a slave named Cato, a group of slaves escaped from their plantation after killing two guards and arming themselves. They headed for Florida and used the beat of drums to rally slaves from other plantations along the way.

After the Cato Conspiracy, slave owners all over the South became very nervous. They feared that slaves from different plantations were using drums to communicate with each other. They knew that some West African peoples used drums in this way. To protect themselves, the frightened slave owners banned the use of drums by their slaves in 1740.

As a result, the slaves had to find new ways to

play the complicated, driving rhythms that were such an important part of their music. People started to invent new sounds. They clicked dried cow-bones or spoons together in fast, rhythmic patterns. They also made rhythms with their mouths, either by chanting words or just using syllables that sounded like drum-beats. They clapped their hands together in a variety of ways and slapped their thighs, chest, and arms to achieve different sounds.

Most important, they tapped rhythms out with their feet. Stomping in rhythm had always been a part of the African dance tradition. Dancers would step in time with the drumbeat. But now drums were outlawed. The rhythms from their feet had to make up for that loss. Not only did their feet need to dance, but also to make the music itself.

After drums were outlawed, African American slaves invented new ways of making rhythm.

Tapping Out the Rhythm

Over the next century and throughout the American Civil War, dancers began to think about the sounds their feet made. They also learned how to change these tones in many ways. Dancers knew that wooden shoes sounded very different from leather ones. They knew that the sound of a clean floor was different from that of a sandy floor. They used this knowledge to make complicated music with only their feet.

By 1865, when the Civil War brought an end to slavery, tap dance was beginning to look like it does today. The best dancers could move their feet as fast as a good drummer could move his hands. Tap traveled up from the South as freed slaves went to cities in the North in search of jobs and a better life.

Learning to tap-dance on the streets became a part of growing up for African American children. They would watch talented dancers challenge each other on street corners and learn from them. Some children were able to supplement the income of their families by dancing. Many parents could not afford to buy their children shoes. But this did not stop these kids from tap dancing. They put bottle caps between their bare toes to make a clicking sound on the sidewalk. Tap dancing had arrived.

Minstrels and the Traveling Show

Minstrels were musicians and entertainers who traveled from town to town across the United States in the nineteenth century. They did performances in tents, called tent shows, in places that had no real theaters. For hundreds of small towns, traveling minstrel shows were the only formal entertainment their citizens ever saw.

By the 1840s, minstrels had become stage performances in which white entertainers imitated African Americans in songs, dances, and comedy skits. These white performers smeared burnt cork over their faces to look like African Americans. This was called blackface. Their distorted portrayal of the way African Americans talked, looked, and danced led to many

This illustration of minstrels performing depicts the exaggerated stereotypes used by whites to portray African Americans.

grotesque stereotypes of African American people.

The popularity of minstrel shows reached its peak between 1850 and 1870. African American dancers were not allowed to share the stage with white dancers. For the most part, minstrel shows were all-male and all-white until after the Civil War, when slavery was abolished. After the war, African Americans began to appear in minstrel shows and often formed their own minstrel companies.

Master Juba

William Henry Lane was a brilliant African American entertainer; his stage name was Master Juba. Juba is a style of rhythm making in which people slap their bodies in intricate patterns. The sound they make takes the place of

Bobby McFerrin, a master of the patting juba style, performing at the Newport Jazz Festival

drum music. Using the body as an instrument in this way is called patting juba. This has been practiced in America since the early nineteenth century. Lane's extraordinary ability to create complicated rhythms with his feet and body made him a famous minstrel.

Spreading Ideas and Sharing Steps

Minstrel shows often featured a competition between two dancers in the tradition of the challenge dances of West Africa. The contenders would stand on a wooden board surrounded by a semicircle of musicians, who accompanied their dancing. Sometimes the musicians used banjos and tambourines. Other times they just clapped, shook rattles, patted juba, or chanted verses in rhythm.

Perhaps the most important thing that minstrel shows did for tap dance was to spread ideas. As minstrels traveled, the styles of various African homelands and different regions of the United States came face to face. This allowed many fine dancers to meet and learn from each other.

African American tap was not the only kind of rhythm dance. Many Irish immigrants came to America in the late nineteenth century because their country was suffering from famine. The Irish had their own distinctive form of rhythm dance, called step dancing. Although it has a completely different style than tap, its fast footwork is just as exciting.

Irish step dancers from the show *Riverdance* performing at the Grammy Awards

Tappers Meet the Irish

As challenge dances became popular, new types began to emerge. Some dances were no longer just between two African American tappers. Instead, one tap dancer and one Irish step dancer would compete. This is how African American tap and Irish step dancing met. Immediately they began to influence one another. Master Juba was one of the first people to combine African dance movements and rhythms with Irish jig steps.

The African American tappers realized the talent of the Irish steppers. Just as European musical styles changed jazz music, Irish jig and English clog dance steps influenced jazz tap. An Irish jig is a lively folk dance. In an English clog dance, a performer wears wooden clogs and taps them against the floor to create a rhythm.

32

African American tap dancers absorbed these European influences and interpreted them in their own unique way. Irish dancers keep their backs straight and their arms at their sides. This style does not fit rhythm tap at all, which favors polyrhythm and flexible body movements. An African American minstrel dancer might borrow a step but do it with a jazzed-up rhythm. He would keep his body loose rather than rigid. He might pulsate his hips and shoulders with the beat. Even though he might use the same step as the Irish dancer, it would have a new quality. For example, when African American dancers began doing clogging steps, the style was called buck wing.

Vaudeville

Vaudeville replaced minstrel shows in the late 1800s. Vaudeville is a kind of theater show featuring a variety of short acts. These acts may include singing, dancing, comedy, and magic routines. People thought that vaudeville was a higher

Four performers from the Ziegfeld Follies, one of the best-known vaudeville troupes

class of entertainment than minstrel shows. Women, who were largely absent from minstrel shows, began to appear in vaudeville. And yet racism against African Americans persisted. They were allowed to perform in white vaudeville theaters only during exclusively African American shows.

White American dancers also wanted to learn African American rhythm dance. They saw that rhythm tap was the most exciting kind of dance in America. But the early period of tap was a hard time for race relations in America.

Segregation

Before the civil rights movement,

segregation existed even in entertainment. Segregation was the racist policy of restricting the access of African Americans to certain places, services, and facilities. This meant that African Americans had their own schools, hospitals, and restaurants, for example. They also performed in separate theaters from whites. African

African Americans had to use a separate rear entrance of this Florida movie house because of segregationist policies.

Bill "Bojangles" Robinson

Bill Robinson, born May 25, 1878, is one of the most important symbols of American rhythm tap. A fantastic dancer, Robinson was the first rhythm tapper to become an international success and one of the first African Americans to become a movie star. With his great talent, belief in himself, and love of people, Robinson became a pioneer of racially integrated entertainment.

Robinson danced first in vaudeville and later in Harlem clubs, Broadway shows, and Hollywood movie musicals. By 1929 he was the highest-paid African American performer in the world. Robinson practiced so much that he wore out twenty to thirty pairs of tap shoes every year. He was most famous for his Stair Dance. Making trombone noises with his mouth, Robinson would trip lightly up and down a specially

made set of wooden stairs. He created more interesting rhythms than most dancers could make on solid ground. One of the best-known images of American tap dance is Bill Robinson teaching his Stair Dance to five-year-old Shirley Temple in the movie *The Little Colonel*.

Long after his death in 1949, Bill "Bojangles" Robinson remains a role model for African Americans.

Americans were not allowed to perform at top venues, working instead in carnivals, tent shows, and clubs. As a result, they were paid less than white performers.

Sometimes, though, the desire of dancers to learn from, compete against, and share moves with each other won out. These desires broke down the separation between African Americans and whites, particularly in tap dancing.

Extraordinary Specialties

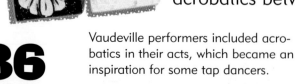

In spite of discrimination, African Americans became the kings and queens of vaudeville dancing. Dance teams such as the Whitman Sisters, a famous all-female touring act, became very popular. Two people with different skills, for example, a pianist and a dancer, made up a dance team. They could play off one another and emphasize each other's skills.

To make it big, a dancer had to have a specialty that was guaranteed to get a great response. Trying to come up with a unique gimmick, tap dancers became very inventive. Some people tapped on suitcases. Some wore roller skates instead of tap shoes. Some even did acrobatics between taps. One tap-

Vaudeville performers included acrobatics in their acts, which became an inspiration for some tap dancers.

per, Earl Tucker, got the name "Snakehips" from his specialty. He would snake his pelvis in traditional African style as he tapped. Elvis Presley, known as "Elvis the Pelvis" in the 1950s, was considered scandalous for doing moves that were very tame compared to those of Snakehips.

One of the great women in vaudeville dance was Ida Forsythe. She was famous for an acrobatic dance style based on a Russian folk step called Kozotsky. Brady Jackson was known as "Jigsaw Jackson, the Human Corkscrew." He would balance the weight of his body on his chin, turning around slowly, while his feet tapped out fast rhythm. And you can just imagine what Henry "Rubberlegs" Williams looked like when he danced!

Minstrel and vaudeville shows helped tap to develop and spread as never before. But these shows could not last forever. As Broadway musicals and Hollywood films became popular, tap had to change with the times.

Elvis and his famous pelvis move

4 movie sets and jazz clubs: tap in the 1920s, '30s, and '40s

Duke Ellington

As tap grew in popularity, many different styles developed. Tap became a part of Broadway musical theater, which was taking over vaudeville. Also, musical comedies were a Hollywood film craze by the 1930s. Tap fit into these films perfectly. It was dance you could not only see but hear.

However, dancing in big theatrical shows and movies was very different from vaudeville. These shows and films were carefully choreographed by the creators, who planned every step in advance. The dancers moved as they were instructed. There was a lot less freedom for creativity.

Some dancers, or hoofers, as they began to be called in the 1920s, adapted their styles to fit the new opportunities. Others preferred to dance in the classy clubs of Harlem in New York City. There they could improvise rhythms and challenge each other as the minstrels did. These dancers spent a lot of time in clubs where jazz musicians performed and were the key to turning tap into jazz tap, which uses tight, rapid footwork to create a rhythmic beat.

On the Broadway Stage

Broadway musicals provided work only for dancers who were willing to come and take their chances in New York City. The competition was even fiercer than it had been in vaudeville. Like vaudeville, many early musicals featured a series of exciting short acts. They also added something that has become a Broadway tap symbol: a chorus line.

Famous dance choreographer Busby Berkeley directing dancers in the musical *42nd Street*

A chorus line was a line of dancers, usually all women, who did the same steps at the same time. Chorus girls were supposed to look alike. They were selected more for their beauty than for their technical skill. They dressed in shiny costumes, kicked their long legs high into the air, stood up very straight, and always wore a big smile. They used tap shoes but danced only very simple rhythms. Using simple rhythms ensured that a large group could keep the same beat. In the 1920s a division began between Broadway tap and rhythm tap. In Broadway tap, the dance's appearance became more important than its sound. People went to shows and movies to see the glamorous costumes and high kicks. The complicated rhythms and body movements of minstrels' rhythm tap were missing. The use of improvisation to

The Rockettes, of New York's Radio City Music Hall, concentrate on performing simple dance steps in perfect unison.

show an individual's unique style and creativity was no longer so important in Broadway tap. Its West African roots were gone. Bill "Bojangles" Robinson was one of the few great dancers who managed to do rhythm tap in musicals and movies.

On the Movie Screen

Unlike rhythm tappers, most Hollywood dancers were not able to improvise. The way filmmakers made tap movies simply did not

Bill "Bojangles" Robinson (left) performs improvisational rhythm tap in the movie *Hol Mikado*.

allow for improvisation. In a tap movie, filmmakers first filmed the dancer. A few days later, they made a sound recording of her taps. A star's dancing often looked a lot better than it sounded.

Take a close look at the dancers the next time an old Hollywood musical is on television. You can hear taps, but no one is wearing tap shoes. That's because the picture was filmed first, and the sound added in later. By wearing other shoes instead of her tap shoes, the dancer was able to make her movements very big.

Swing—A Brand-New Dance

Meanwhile, back in Harlem, New York City, tap dance and jazz music began to grow together and influence each other. As a result, in the late 1920s a style of jazz called swing emerged. It was characterized by a steady and lively rhythm with improvisation. Swing, sometimes called

Swing Dancers

big band music, was often performed by a large band of about fifteen members. The consistent beat of this music inspired dancers to develop faster footwork and new body movements.

Duke Ellington (at the piano) and his big band of jazz musicians played upbeat music that inspired dancers.

The nightclubs of Harlem brought a new level of racial integration. At the Savoy Ballroom, dances that had begun in Europe were becoming popular with African Americans, who developed and changed them. Dances such as the Charleston and the lindy, later known as the jitterbug, were the rage among young people of all races. People, black and white, considered going to the Cotton Club to hear Duke Ellington or Count Basie play jazz to be the height of stylish city life. Often a big band performed with a tap dancer.

A dance enthusiast performing some acrobatic moves at the Savoy Ballroom, "Home of the Happy Feet"

BeBop—A Brand-New Jazz

A new kind of jazz began in New York in the 1940s. Charlie Parker, the great saxophone player known as Bird, was one of the inventors of a brand of jazz called bebop. Bebop got its name from its unusual sounds and rhythms. In swing music, the kind of jazz that was popular before bebop, the rhythms were consistent and

seemed to move easily from one phrase to another. The musicians who invented bebop did not want their music to sound that agreeable. They added accents in the rhythm that made the beat jagged and surprising. Saying the word "bebop" gives some idea of the feel of that style of music.

Hoofers in the 1940s may have been the real inventors of bebop rhythms. Some people think that musicians took the idea from dance. In truth, the dancers and musicians probably influenced each other.

Pianists, sax players, and trumpeters played jagged, unexpected notes. At the same time, drummers and tap dancers experimented with new ideas of rhythm and phrasing. All this activity led to the creation of bebop.

Hoofers

Tough Competition

The growing jazz tap scene in New York and on the West Coast was brimming with remarkable talent. Tap was growing in many different directions at once.

Famous tap dancer Gregory Hines in a challenge with some of his mentors. The other dancers pictured include (from left to right): Arthur Duncan, Pat Rico, Harold Nicholas, Steve Condos, Sandman Sims, Henry LeTang, and Sammy Davis Jr.

The many great dancers are too numerous to mention. During this time, dancers were each other's strongest support, toughest competition, and best teachers. There was no official school for jazz tap dance. Young people had to learn by watching other dancers. Young tap dancers would come to New York to learn from and show their stuff to the old masters. As in tap's African tradition, dancers got new ideas from challenging each other. Challenges brought out each dancer's best steps, which took years of practice to perfect. They motivated dancers to show off their individual styles. Sandman Sims once said, "Dancing is competitive, like fighting." Life as a hoofer was not easy. Only a prizefighter in rhythm could survive.

45

In the 1950s rock and roll music and dances like the twist swept the nation, and the popularity of jazz tap began to dwindle.

5 learning and celebrating tap: today and tomorrow

By the 1950s rock and roll had taken over popular music in the United States. Rock and roll was exciting, loud, and energetic. Its simple electric beat was easy to move to and easy to hear. Like jazz tap, rock has African roots. Soon everyone in the United States was doing dances like the twist, based on African body movement. However, rock and roll did not have the right feel for rhythm tap. As a result, jazz tap's popularity declined.

Many tap dancers found themselves out of work. Some took other jobs, figuring it was time to hang up their shoes. A few found ways to make a living through dance. For example, one tapper, Cholly Atkins, worked teaching the Temptations and other Motown groups to do those slick, synchronized steps that you see in their

Cholly Atkins

videos from the 1960s. It was a living, but the 1950s and '60s were hard times for hoofers.

The Tap Revival

Fortunately, a new generation rediscovered tap. When people became interested in tap again in the late 1970s, many of the great master tappers from the 1940s were still alive. They were healthy enough to dance and teach.

Savion Glover is teaching tap to a whole new generation of dancers.

In the 1970s, younger tappers like Jane Goldberg and Brenda Bufalino in New York led a movement to seek out the old African American hoofers. They wanted them to teach their valuable skills and secrets. By the 1980s many tap dancers who thought that they would never perform again were teaching and dancing all over the world.

Filmmaker George Nierenberg made excellent video documentaries that recorded the wisdom of the old masters along with tales of their struggles and achievements. Gregory Hines, a famous tapper who has appeared in numerous Broadway shows and films,

Gregory Hines performing in the movie *Tap*

also promoted traditional rhythm tap. His movie *Tap* features many of the best dancers of the 1940s doing a challenge dance, just as in the old vaudeville days. The efforts of many students and the dedication of the old masters revived tap.

Breakdancing became the urban street dance of the 1980s.

Tap Dancing Meets Street Dancing

You no longer can learn to tap-dance by hanging out on city streets. However, African Americans still have a street dance tradition. For example, breakdancing is a form that began on city streets. It is usually performed to rap music and involves acrobatics and difficult floor movements, such as spinning on your back or head. Challenge dances are a common feature of break dancing. Each dancer enters a circle and shows his best moves, trying to outdo his rivals. Break dancing, funk, and hip hop are all modern dance styles with African roots.

African American dance has many new influences.

However, you can still see many similarities between new and old dance forms. The late tap master Charles Honi Coles could remember vaudeville performers that did Kozotsky dancing. Kozotsky actually looked a lot like break dancing. It used head spins, hand spins, slow splits, and chin stands—all done in formal evening wear. The moonwalk, popularized by Michael Jackson, is a move that tap dancers were doing in Harlem in the 1920s. Tap dance is the original street dance.

Today tap dancers are exploring the connection between tap and other forms of street dance. Savion Glover, one of the brightest young stars of tap dancing, is very interested in this connection. He often works with children, appearing frequently on the television show *Sesame Street*. As a result, Glover can influence the coming generation of tap dancers. He talks tap in a street dance language that young people understand. He also has two of the fastest feet on the planet, which makes everyone stop and listen. Glover and other dancers are combining tap dance with street dance to create new and exciting styles.

Savion Glover performing in the Broadway musical *Bring in 'da Noise, Bring in 'da Funk*

The Future of Tap Dance

Tap is becoming more like the music on MTV. It is getting plugged in, electrified, and synthesized. For example, Alfred Desio in California has developed a system called TapTronics, or Zapped Taps. With TapTronics he can turn a pair of tap shoes into electronic music.

Computers and synthesizers are now being used to give tap a more electrified sound.

By inserting a device between each tap and the sole of the shoe, Desio can put tap sounds through a synthesizer. He can make his taps sound like a drum machine, metallic crashes, echoes, squeaks, chirps, or even musical chords. A system called digital sampling allows Desio to make a recording of something (for example, his own voice) and then make that sound

51

come out of his shoes. Gregory Hines made TapTronics famous in his 1989 movie *Tap*. Savion Glover agrees that electronic tapping is the wave of the future. It uses an old dance form to make new sounds and to attract young people.

Not everyone chooses electricity to add new dimensions to tap dancing. There are as many innovative ideas as there are tap dancers.

Paul Draper combined tap and ballet.

Jane Goldberg has combined tap dancing with comedy.

Leon Collins, Fred Strickler, and others have popularized tapping to classical music.

Brenda Bufalino works with African-style polyrhythms.

Anita Feldman has invented the Tap Dance Instrument, a wood and metal structure that makes a different tone depending upon where she taps on it.

Gregory Hines has been working to reconnect the styles of Broadway and rhythm tap.

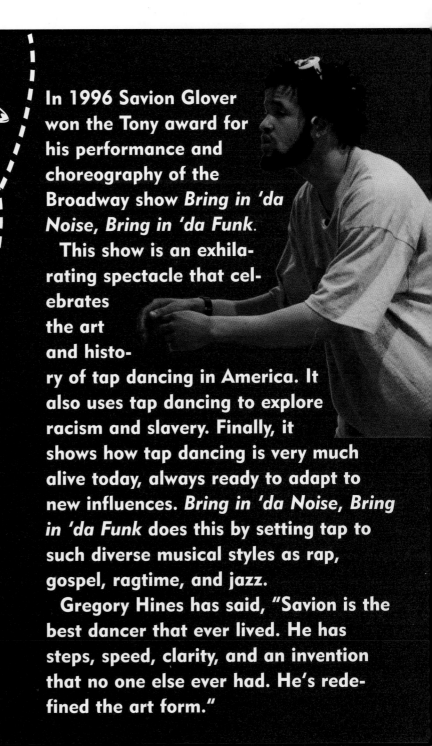

In 1996 Savion Glover won the Tony award for his performance and choreography of the Broadway show *Bring in 'da Noise, Bring in 'da Funk*.

This show is an exhilarating spectacle that celebrates the art and history of tap dancing in America. It also uses tap dancing to explore racism and slavery. Finally, it shows how tap dancing is very much alive today, always ready to adapt to new influences. *Bring in 'da Noise, Bring in 'da Funk* does this by setting tap to such diverse musical styles as rap, gospel, ragtime, and jazz.

Gregory Hines has said, "Savion is the best dancer that ever lived. He has steps, speed, clarity, and an invention that no one else ever had. He's redefined the art form."

Hordes of people tap their way across town on New York's 34th Street during Macy's annual Tap-O-Mania Sunday.

These are just a few of the most influential new ideas in tap. In general, tap dancers are trying to learn even more about music; they want to work more closely with musicians. They are also studying the roots of tap. Some tappers have been teaming up with African drummers to explore the rhythmic connections between these two forms.

It is important both to innovate in tap and to keep the beautiful old traditions alive. Tap is no longer in danger of dying out. People from all over the world come to America to study this rich dance form with the great masters. Concert tap touring companies and tap festivals are drawing huge crowds. There is even an International Tapdance Association, so fans can always find out what's happening in every part of the tapping globe. America celebrates National Tap Dance Day every spring on May 25, Bill "Bojangles" Robinson's birthday.

A Proud Tradition Lives On

Jazz tap dance has a long, proud tradition. It began as the voice of a people who had no other voice. African slaves used the dance styles and rhythms of their homeland to create a new musical form. As African Americans struggled to gain freedom, their dancing grew and spread. On its journey it exchanged ideas with other dance cultures it met along the way. Now tap has grown to be one of the most exciting, adaptable, long lasting dance forms in the world. People of all cultures and lands are learning the joy of making music with their shoes and dancing out the rhythms in their hearts.

The tradition of tap will continue to live and grow in new generations of dancers.

bebop   Style of jazz characterized by a jagged and surprising beat.

break dancing   Dance style usually performed to rap music that involves acrobatics and difficult floor movements.

Broadway tap   Also called show tap; style of tap dance that emphasizes the presentation and arrangement of steps.

challenge dance   African tradition in which dancers compete with each other.

choreography   Composition and arrangement of dance steps.

chorus line   Line of dancers who do the same steps at the same time.

improvisation   Acting spontaneously or without a set routine.

minstrel   Musician or entertainer who traveled from town to town.

pantomime   Movement that imitates something, usually an animal.

plantation   Very large farm; many used slaves as laborers.

polyrhythm   Use of more than one rhythm at the same time.

rhythm   Musical pattern of regularly recurring sounds or beats.

segregation   Racist policy of restricting the access of African Americans to certain places, services, and facilities.

swing   Style of jazz characterized by a steady, lively rhythm with improvisation.

vaudeville   Theater show featuring a variety of short acts.

About Tap. Directed by George T. Nierenberg. Narrated by Gregory Hines. Los Angeles: Direct Cinema, Ltd., 28 minutes (1984).

Dancing: New World, New Forms. Created by Rhoda Grauer. Hosted and narrated by Raoul Trujillo. Chicago: Home Vision. Part of the 8-videocassette, 464-minute series *Dancing* (1993).

Great Feats of Feet. Directed by Brenda Bufalino (1967).

Let's Tap. Directed by Dave Hilmer. Produced by Marilyn Shapiro. Los Angeles: Karl Lorimar Home Video, 90 minutes (1984).

Masters of Tap. Directed by Jolyon Wilmhurst. Produced by Charles Thompson. Chicago: Home Vision, 61 minutes (1983).

No Maps on My Taps. Directed by George T. Nierenberg. New York: GTN Productions. Two film reels, 59 minutes (1978).

Songs Unwritten: A Tap Dancer Remembered: The Life and Legacy of Leon Collins. Written, produced, and directed by David Wadsworth. Narrated by Will Lyman. Philadelphia, PA: Leon Collins Archive, 58 minutes (1988).

Tap. Directed by Nick Castle. Starring Gregory Hines and Sammy Davis Jr. Burbank, CA: Columbia Tri-Star Home Video, 110 minutes (1989).

Tap Dogs. Directed by Nigel Triffitt. Beverly Hills, CA: 20th Century Fox Home Entertainment, 73 minutes (1997).

Where to Learn More about Jazz Tap

American Tap Dance Orchestra, Inc. (ATDO)
463 West Street
Apt. H525
New York, NY 10014
(212) 243-6438

Chicago Human Rhythm Project (CHRM) .
1319 West Granville
2nd floor
Chicago, IL 60660-1910
(773) 761-4889
Web Site: http://www.humanrhythmproject.com
e-mail: CHRProject@aol.com

International Tap Association
P.O. Box 356
Boulder, CO 80306
(303) 443-7989
Web Site: http://www.tapdance.org/tap/ita
e-mail: intertap@cocentric.net

Los Angeles Choreographers and Dancers
351 South Virgil Avenue
Los Angeles, CA 90020
(213) 385-1171
Web Site: http://www.usc.edu/dept/dance/p2_lacd.html
e-mail: louisehr@mizar.usc.edu

Rhapsody in Taps
Artistic Director, Linda Sohl-Donnell
4812 Matney Avenue
Long Beach, CA 90807
Web Site: http://www.performingarts.net/Shafman/Rhapsody/index.html

Web Sites

http://www.dancemagazine.com
http://www.isratap.co.il/
http://www.tapdance.org/tap/
http://www.tapdogs.com

For Further reading

Feldman, Anita. *Inside Tap: Technique and Improvisation for Today's Tap Dancer.* Pennington, NJ: Princeton Book Company, 1996.

Frank, Rusty E., and Gregory Hines. *Tap: The Greatest Tap Dance Stars and Their Stories, 1900–1955.* New York: Da Capo, 1995.

Haskins, James. *Black Dance in America: A History Through Its People.* New York: HarperCollins, 1992.

Knowles, Mark. *The Tap Dance Dictionary.* Jefferson, NC: McFarland, 1998.

Ormonde, Jimmy. *Tap Dancing at a Glance.* Bedford, MA: Applewood, 1996.

Stearns, Marshall Winslow. *Jazz Dance: The Story of American Vernacular Dance.* New York: Da Capo, 1994.

Credits

Acknowledgments

With love, to the American Tap Dance Orchestra

The editors wish to thank Linda Sohl-Donnell, dancer and artistic director of Rhapsody in Taps, for her expert review of the manuscript.

About the Author

While at the University of Wisconsin-Madison to earn a bachelor's degree in Greek and Latin languages, Johnson studied jazz tap with Donna Pecket. In 1991 she moved to New York City. There she studied as an apprentice with Brenda Bufalino and the American Tap Dance Orchestra (ATDO). Johnson has worked with the ATDO as a percussionist and musical arranger. She also has performed her own tap choreography in New York City. Through graduate work in classical music theory, Johnson hopes to combine her love of music, scholarship, and writing.

Photo Credits

Cover photo by Michal Daniel; pp. 2, 4 © AP/ Associated Press; p. 7 © Archive Photos/ American Stock; p 8-9 © AP/ Associated Press/Ahmanson Theater; pp. 10-11, 18, 37 (bottom left), 49 © CORBIS/UPI; pp. 13, 21, 24, 29, 33, 35 (bottom left), 42, 46, 50, 55 © Archive Photos; p.14 © CORBIS/ Otto Lang; pp. 16, 35 (top right), 40, 43, 45, 48 (top right), 53, 54 © AP/ Wide World Photos; pp. 17, 20, 38, 39, 41, 42, 43, 44, 47, 48 (bottom left) © The Everett Collection; pp. 23, 25, 27, 34, 36, 51 © CORBIS; p. 28 © Michal Daniel; p.30 © Chick Harrity/ CORBIS; p. 37 (top right) © Archive Photos/ Frank Driggs Collection; pp. 31, 32 © Reuters/Fred Prouser/Archive Photos

Design and Layout

Laura Murawski

Consulting Editors

Erin M. Hovanec and Erica Smith